Pure Lizard

SUJATA BHATT was born in Ahmedabad, India. She grew up in Pune (India) and in the United States. She received her MFA from the Writers' Workshop at the University of Iowa. To date, she has published six collections of poetry with Carcanet Press. She received the Commonwealth Poetry Prize (Asia) and the Alice Hunt Bartlett Award for her first collection, *Brunizem* (1988). Subsequent collections include *Monkey Shadows* (PBS recommendation, 1991), *The Stinking Rose* (shortlisted for the Forward Poetry Prize, 1995), *Point No Point* (1997), *Augatora* (PBS Recommendation, 2000), and *A Colour for Solitude* (2002). She received a Cholmondeley Award in 1991 and the Italian Tratti Poetry Prize in 2000. She has translated Gujarati poetry into English for the *Penguin Anthology of Contemporary Indian Women's Poetry*, and has translated poems by Günter Grass and Günter Kunert. Her translations from the German include *Mickle Makes Muckle: poems, mini plays and short prose* by Michael Augustin (Dedalus Press, 2007). She has been a Lansdowne Visiting Writer at the University of Victoria, in British Columbia, a Visiting Fellow at Dickinson College in Pennsylvania, and more recently was Poet-in-Residence at the Poetry Archive in London. Her work has been widely anthologised, broadcast on radio and television, and has been translated into more than twenty languages. Currently, Sujata Bhatt lives in Germany with her husband and daughter.

Also by Sujata Bhatt from Carcanet Press

Brunizem
Monkey Shadows
The Stinking Rose
Point No Point: Selected Poems
Augatora
A Colour for Solitude

SUJATA BHATT

Pure Lizard

CARCANET

Acknowledgements

Thanks are due to the editors of the following publications in which some of these poems, sometimes in different versions, first appeared: *Kavya Bharati* (India); *Carapace* (South Africa); *Tabacaria* (Portugal); *Amastra-N-Gallar* (Galicia, Spain); *Poetry London, PN Review, Poetry Review* (UK); *The Harrisburg Review, Sirena* (USA); *The Malahat Review* (Canada); *Summer Solstice 2007, Days of Poetry, Skopelos Festival Anthology* (Greece).

An earlier version of 'In the End' first appeared in *We Have Come Through*, edited by Peter Forbes (Bloodaxe, 2003). 'Gale Force Winds' and 'Living with Stones' were commissioned and broadcast by BBC Radio Drama as a part of the series 'With Love from Me to You', a literary correspondence with the Welsh poet Gillian Clarke. 'What is Exotic?' has been included in the Oxfam CD *Life Lines 2*, edited by Todd Swift, and produced in 2007.

Special thanks to Rolf Wienbeck for the cover drawing, created exclusively for this book. Thanks also, to Paola Splendore and Andrea Sirotti for translating some of these poems into Italian, to Hasso Krull for translations into Estonian, to Jorge Sagastume for translations into Spanish, to Mi-Sun Mun for translations into Korean, and to Michael Augustin for translations into German.

Additional thanks are due to Dickinson College (Carlisle, Pennsylvania) for a Visiting Fellowship during the academic year 2003–4, to the British Council in Rome, to the Poetry Archive in London, and to the Korea Translation Literature Institute in Seoul.

For their comments and advice regarding this manuscript, I am immensely grateful to Elke Durden, Chris Gribble, Jenny Leach, Bharat Pathak, Victoria Sams, Michael Schmidt, and Eleanor Wilner.

First published in Great Britain in 2008 by
Carcanet Press Limited
Alliance House
Cross Street
Manchester M2 7AQ

A CIP catalogue record for this book is available from the British Library
ISBN 978 1 85754 833 4

The publisher acknowledges financial assistance from Arts Council England

Typeset in Bembo by XL Publishing Services, Tiverton
Printed and bound in England by SRP Ltd, Exeter

for Michael and Jenny Mira Swantje

and for Jenny Leach
(25th November 1948–19th August 2007)

We drop Cassandra's mantle in the dust.
The king will not return. The king is dead.
And look: the olives ripen, the lizards stretch.
Eleanor Wilner

Contents

I

A Hidden Truth

A Hidden Truth

Those three monkeys:
      see no evil
      hear no evil
      speak no evil —
actually wear kimonos.
Tomorrow,
      they'll wear saris.
Truth stays hidden —
it lives within their hands,
within their palms which are
so burnt —   and scarred
      into a violent purple.

Those three monkeys:
      see no evil
      hear no evil
      speak no evil —
They always knew
they were women —
Women, not monkeys.
And one day the camera
revealed their souls.

The Fourth Monkey

The fourth monkey has been forgotten,
despite her golden face, her golden hands,
stained red from staunching the world's blood.

How could you forget?

Don't you know?
She tried to cleanse Lady Macbeth.

She is, after all, do no evil.

Well then, find a place for her
with see no evil, hear no evil and speak no evil.

But let her speak.
Listen. She says:

'Don't bind me for a touch of Asia,
                    a touch of Africa –

I have the full DNA.'

Two Monkeys

'That's quite a feat,
to escape from a crocodile
        with your liver intact,'

says one monkey to another,
as they eat chapattis,
chapattis stolen from a cat.

'Escape, escape!
That's the whole point of my life.
It would be boring otherwise.'

'Must we behave like monkeys?'
Second monkey continues.
'Can't we learn something else?'

The Crow, his Beak and a Girl

How this crow keeps his beak full –
He knows where to dance.

He follows a girl, a child of three,
across her grandmother's garden.

The girl is so thin, and she runs
with a hot chapatti in one hand,
      and a doll in the other –

The crow is close behind her.
They zigzag through the spider lilies.

Soon the crow flies off
      with the chapatti.

And he's there again the next day,
      and the next –

And he always flies off with the chapatti.

The first time is a shock for the girl –
      the suddenness,
the dusty black wings flapping so close to her face –

But then she gets used to it,
      stops fearing his beak,
   which rarely touches her anyway.
Now she simply watches –
stares at the other crows
      who aren't so brave.

Nine Poems in Response to Etchings by Paula Rego

The Crow's House

They've stayed up all night
            on the sofa,
in this crow's house –
and now it's grey morning.

The maid won't let the blackbird leave.
The white cat is dizzy with disease.

A black dog has lost control
of his neck muscles.

Suddenly, three holy ghosts
appear in the background –
They've fled from Lübeck
and now they want to work together.
They want to be innocent
            heralds of peace –
And yet, they ignore the fallen baby,
the bald, newly hatched head
            with a beak,
unable to lift itself up,
unable to do anything but cry –

But the crow won't
      meet anyone's gaze today.

The Crow and his Cat

How this crow loves his cat –
A cat who is whiter than milk.

She is so lean and hungry –
but he's even hungrier.

His beak will pierce her throat
            any second.

He'll call it an accident,
he'll call it fate —
        a self-fulfilling prophesy.

Meanwhile, his white cat lies
on her back and imagines
another sort of feasting.

A Tube of Paint

A crow sits with his tube of paint —
        black paint.

Triumphant, fulfilled —
he has just turned his white cats
into tiger cats — he has poured
some of his blackness
                into their stripes.

What fun he had holding the brush
        in his beak.
He turned his head from side to side,
twirling the bristles
across their fur — he could feel their bones
against each stroke —
and oh how their muscles
        and ligaments quivered —

'Don't be afraid!' he cried —
'Soon these black stripes will swirl
something more into your blood —
and you'll be able to understand me.'

But the cats are afraid.
They're still kittens,
in the last months of their kittenish moods.
And so they cower behind the crow —
        waiting for a chance
            to run away —

The Night Crow

This crow knows the stars
are his discarded eyes.

Every day
   when he awakens
he opens new eyes.

And every night
his old eyes are flung
far out into the skies.

This crow knows
starlight comes from his own voice
which has trapped the sun.

Of course, he shines brighter
         than those stars:
his discarded eyes –

Sewing on the Shadow

Always on a full moon –
   month after month
he comes to her window,
   chasing his shadow –

Always on a full moon
he asks Wendy to sew it back on.

He thinks there's no blood involved –
He feels no pain.
He believes the thread is invisible.

But Wendy sees every stitch
before her – reddened with blood –
and her own blood flows faster –

She's sewing a riddle on to his skin,
a code only she can decipher.

And every month as she sews
an egg ripens within her –

And every month she wonders
whether the bleeding will begin
                                on time –

Flying Children

The sky is washed blue,
                    Araucana blue.

The sky is a giant egg
    opening to swallow children.

And, of course, the children wanted to fly.

Wendy is the calmest.
She has just glimpsed her future
growing on the other side
    of the garden. And now she knows
she has nothing to fear.

She'll just keep flying through
                    these innocent years,
Her face, not quite anywhere,
        but dreaming of the future –
            Yes, her entire face,
eyes, nose, mouth, muscles,
        dreaming, waiting –

Wendy and the Lost Boys

Wendy wears lavender
when she plays mother –
Her fingers grow gentle,
her face has changed.

She wears a long white apron
like a nurse or a cook –
and in her hair, a red ribbon
because she's still a girl.

She hums to herself
becoming the essence of lavender –
Tall, slender –
the wind runs through her.

Even her face takes on
the expression of lavender.
Oh, she'll never be a tiger lily,
she never wanted to be such a warrior.

But oh how the lost boys love her,
love her for being lavender.
They're waiting for their clothes, their shoes –
they're waiting for Wendy, for milk and honey.

The lost boys have become so small,
they can barely walk. They crawl around Wendy,
(like babies, not crocodiles) they need her
to lift them up and hold them tight.

And Wendy keeps smiling
because she knows her power, her strength.
All these boys will listen to her –
but she'll escape before they touch her heart.

Mermaid Drowning Wendy

From a distance
   this mermaid
looks like a seal.
But when you get closer
you can see
she's an old woman.

She's the oldest
mermaid in Neverland –
and she wants to kill Wendy.

Wendy has everything
the mermaid wants:
Innocence and beauty
and a pure heart.

A pure heart
pumping real blood.

The mermaid cannot
   bear it any longer.

Drowning is such a gentle
way to go, the mermaid thinks –
a silky slide to Death.

And what's so bad
  about dying?
After all, the mermaid herself
   is already dead.

Wendy's Song

Wendy couldn't wait
    to have babies –
and now she's on her way.

She's such a good mother
that other babies, even foetuses
have flocked to her house.

Now she's not sure
she wants so many.
Still, she'll try to feed them.
She plans to grow something else
besides roses in her garden.

Meanwhile, she stirs her soup –
a soup of blood
in a pot the size of a bucket.
It's the blood of her anger
    where foetuses lie
      submerged.

She must keep stirring
so it doesn't stick to the bottom.

She wants to find
    a use for it –
A purpose
    for this rich blood.

II

Telemann's Frogs

What is Exotic?

for Hasso Krull

Sweden is exotic –
and so is all of Finland.

Whortleberries certainly are.

Estonia is exotic –
and so is the Estonian word
for lizard: *sisalik.*

But the lizard herself
is my sister – those hot afternoons
when she comes indoors
                to hide –

Pure Lizard

She is
part lizard, part woman,
and one of her ancestors
must have been a monkey.

Her skin is pure lizard.
Perhaps she's also part chameleon.
Her eyes are tiny. Her face is
                narrow, angular.

I am four in this memory,
four when I see her
            standing on a wall –
There's a crowd listening to her.
She can even speak Marathi.
She's just as tall as I am –
but so old, and her skin hangs
everywhere from the bones in her body.

I think she is a hairless monkey –
and I want to get closer
            to listen, to speak to her.

I want her to tell me everything
                about monkeyhood.
I want to see if she actually
                has a tail.
I want to play hide-and-seek
                with her.

Now, what is she telling the people?
She is shrill, crying out to them.

There is so much anguish
rippling across her skin –
such desperation in her voice.
And yet, some people are laughing.
I want to know why –

but I am pulled away,
told that it's time to go home.

I thought of her again today,
    still certain of my memory.

Who was she? Who is she?
  Where is she now − ?

My very own Sybil −

Storm

The Goddess at your heels –

Her sari: a yellow storm.

Birds abandon you.

You're on your own now
    with her.

Even if she speaks
    to you in anger,
you are blessed.

Bhagavati

On the train from Madurai
to Thiruvananthapuram – how I wait
for the flashes of red earth
        between the endless green
        of the coconut trees.

How I think of you, Bhagavati –

Here, the earth spills
        bright red from a gash
in a hill – there a field is slashed deep enough
for the red to show.

Where are you now?
Have you become
        the soul of one of these trees?
They say the Goddess lives here –
        could it also be you?

Look, everywhere the trees are turning
        greener, darker –
as if they want to hide in the thickening sky,
as if they too will shift to indigo.

I want to learn this all by heart,
I want to understand the shape of the light.

The train rushes on faster
and faster – so there is a breeze,
so even the monsoon air
        turns a bit cooler.

But I would like to slow down
Bhagavati, I would stop this train
at least a hundred times between stations.

Bhagavati, how were you named?
Why did your mother

name you Bhagavati? You were born
and your mother thought 'Bhagavati' –
Was it so simple? Perhaps she wanted you
to be strong, even fierce – you were already
beautiful – Perhaps she wanted the Goddess
to keep you safe –

You were sixteen years old
when they married you off to an older man
who took you to America –
How could your mother know
about the tumour
that would grow in your liver –
You were twenty-seven, maybe twenty-eight –
with three children: two boys and the youngest
a girl, barely a year old.
Who could imagine it was a tumour
that made you sick?
I remember chopping radishes
in your kitchen – fat red ones, so slippery
and so round – thinner and thinner
I chopped them – It was a game
to see how fast I could move the knife,
how thin I could make the slices, until the red
disappeared into slivers: wet threads of silk around
            the spicy white disks –

I was only fourteen then,
but I knew you didn't want more children –
knew how you begged to have your tubes tied.
            I knew you feared
your husband – how you protected your children
from him – In the end
you always spoke to my mother
on the telephone, when the children
were at school – yours and hers –
In the end the doctors cut the tumour out
from your liver – In the end that was all
they could do – In the end we visited you
in hospital and the first thing

you said was 'good-bye'.
In the end the doctors could not explain
what caused the tumour to grow – although
there were studies already
connecting the Pill to liver cancer – In the end
my mother was convinced it was the Teflon, non-stick
coating on your pots and pans that got mixed
up with your food and poisoned your liver.
In the end you sent for your sister –
She was my age – and she hardly spoke to anyone.
Remember?
You were the age of my mother's sister
and I was the same age as yours – another circle –
                              remember?

In the end
you went back to Rajasthan
to die in your parents' home –

Bhagavati, the fields are full
        with young plantain leaves.
It is the brightest green I have seen in a long time –
Your daughter must be almost twenty-nine now –
They say the Goddess lives here –
But don't ask me why –
don't ask me why I think of you today
on my way to Kerala –
Don't ask me why
I like to repeat your name, Bhagavati.

Coffee

The signs are mostly in Tamil
at this tiny railway station.

It is the time between sunset
and a completely black monsoon sky.

And then the vendors come, walking
back and forth along the platform
            beside this train.

'Coffee, coffee, coffee, coffee...'
an old man cries out – even as I buy
a cup and then another –
'Coffee, coffee, coffee, coffee...'
through the bars of the window.

He doesn't bargain, doesn't raise his price –
Trusts the amount I give is correct.
Wait, wait! I'm about to say, don't trust me, don't
trust anyone – But there he goes –

'Coffee, coffee, coffee, coffee...' he continues
calling as if he lived beyond this world already –

He stares ahead, looking somewhere
into the distance, beyond the train –

And I look at his dazed eyes: red, feverish –
            yet strangely focused –
and his eyelids: red, swollen –
but still, his face is quiet – yes,
            it is a small, quiet face.

He looks at the sky
as if he's searching for something.

Clouds move slowly,
      sliding across each other

like large beasts,
  still sluggish as they awaken
from a deep sleep –

The clouds move further and further apart –
  And suddenly: stars –
stars of such brightness
 as if they're on fire, as if
they'll explode
   any moment –

He looks at the sky –

Who knows what he believes.
Who knows what starlight means to him.

Good Omens

Milk of green coconuts
    we drank this morning –

Milk of green coconuts –

Like drinking the earliness
    of morning, the clarity –

How can the body
    understand its soul?

How can the soul
    be so patient
with its body?

We drove far out
    of Ahmedabad
on our way to the step well –

What is the meaning
    of a journey?

And then
it was already noon –
    and then,
how we rushed in, running
    down steps to the well – Deeper

and deeper – the smell
    of moss filling our lungs –
a cool wetness – sudden darkness –

I clung to pillars
    leaned back against walls –
So afraid of falling in –

We peered down
at thick water
    peeling itself away, away –

Already shrunken puddles
    wanting to be gone –

How this water foamed –

    A sob, a greenish black noise –

We imagined a time
when people came here
for water that was fragrant –
    almost salty, almost sweet
like Ahmedabad water –

A time of plenty,
    of innocence –
A time without oppressors –

When I climbed out
    stepping into the sun,
a peacock flew up into a tree
    on the other side of the road –
Such a tall tree for a peacock –

His long tail, especially long,
    hung down – brushing against
dusty air, across large dark leaves
    swollen with humidity –

His tail so thick with feathers,
    their curved edges
frayed here and there,
    curled like huge eyelashes
over those eyes –
    those startled eyes –

Feathers ruffled, flowing
yet almost electric
    with monsoon static –

His tail so heavy
        almost pleated together –
glistening violet, black, violet – like silk –
    then sparkling blue with shadows
of burnished green – all the gold hidden
but still flashing out now and then
as he moved from branch to branch
            uncertain, restless –
But letting us watch him
        for so many minutes
before he flew somewhere
further away between other trees –

And we too turned
        another way –

We walked as if
our souls were threatening to leave
    our bodies right here – as if Truth
had suddenly appeared in every molecule
around us – and we could not go –

What is the meaning
        of a journey?

Sometimes we stand
and look at each other
and say nothing, nothing –

Like blood glistening over a wound –
The healing, invisible –

How long it has taken me
    to speak of this –

How does one continue?
How shall I – ?

And what about the tangents
    the detours?

Before we left
you showed me the banyan tree
    I had forgotten –
The banyan tree
      not far from the well –
A tree so old, it has always
      been here, you said –
So many vines and trunks –
    branches becoming shoots
and new trunks – such a cluster –
    a shelter –
And then, that gesture we have
of standing before the tree
        close up –
and looking way up at the sky beyond it –
that gesture of touching it
    as if we want to memorise
banyan bark – and then stroking the vines,
patting the trunks, as if
    we were greeting
a group of elephants –

Only the Blackest Stones

To get here
you have to climb through
hills where the fiercest monkeys live.
You will see flashes of sunlight,
the wind rippling across
    their honey-brown fur –
And you might watch, entranced –
but they will descend screaming, enraged,
they will chase you away
    rushing you on to the snakes –

And if you worry
    about where to step
you will never find your way.

Over here
only the blackest stones
can become snakes –
    cobras – little kings –
some lie almost asleep beneath trees –
their heads moulded into sleekness,
such gentleness curled into the grass –
Others rise up, hoods flared
as if to say, welcome, welcome –
    but beware –
They rise up
and yet, they are frozen
forever in that poise.

Nearby, an old man sits
waiting for coins, for an offering of fruit –
waiting for someone who needs
    to be blessed –

What will you say to him?
    What will you do?

Cloth dolls hang

from these trees above the snakes:
     finger-sized flowers –
Here and there
          tiny cradles dangle –
     green and pink prayers –
dusty, dusty – even this faded
yellow cloth, a faceless thing
tied to a branch, begs for children
to be born – many children –
                         many –

Further up – there's another path
where steps lead to a terrace –
And if you enter
          you are filled
with the solitude of snakes –
               you are surrounded –
Their black stone skins
breathe in the heat – turmeric stained
          they stare at you
and their souls pulse gold –

Despite the density of stone
their souls are almost liquid,
their souls are egg yolks –
round, firm, slippery gold
deep inside – somewhere
     there is movement
insects breathing across leaves –
a throbbing – as their blackness
          absorbs the heat –

Sometimes
if you look away
at the sky – you can find
the words your mind needs
against this silence –

Turmeric stained
          stone snakes –

they stare at you
        as if ready to listen –

A small girl breaks the silence –
she calls out to her father
and starts running –
She zigzags between the snakes,
running across the terrace –
        circling one way
and then another –
Her thin arms moving fast,
bones jutting out of her elbows –
        She doesn't stop.

Parvati Temple, Poona

Once upon a time... so the story goes,
a girl of two ran up the steps
on the hill where Parvati sits.
She ran up so fast, even her mother
couldn't keep up –
Luckily, someone stopped the child
before she reached the top, before
she reached Parvati – and told her
to wait for her mother.
I think of this story
as I climb the steps today
knowing it was about my own
mother who had lost her daughter.
And in my mind I can hear
my mother's voice saying:
'Don't you remember? I always
took you there – Yes, also
when you were older.'
Today it's still early – still
the coolest part of the day.
No one is here – except
for the joggers, racing up and down, they are
so oblivious to the view.
It is my second day in Poona
after so many years – and I am
not oblivious. I can sit with Parvati
for a long time. I can look into
her stern eyes and wish for more dreams,
more journeys – And then,
when I stand up and turn around
I can admire Nandi's black stone skin
                forever –
While Memory laughs in my face
saying: 'I dare you, I dare you
                to remember – '

Whenever I Return

Whenever I return to this garden
I am ten or eleven –
　　Sometimes even twelve
but never older –

This time, I come alone.

I find the corner
　　　where I always sat:
a slab of stone beside leafy bushes.
From there I watched
everyone come and go –

　　Equidistant
from neem tree and tamarind tree
　　I stayed.

No one has died yet –
　　no one is sick.

The ground is cooler here.
Dragonflies skim over me –
sometimes touch my hair
　　　　sometimes
brush against my face –

I don't need to count
the flowers – I know
they are all there – even if
they are still seeds, still hard
waiting inside the ground –
or even if they are already cut
and taken by my mother –

On days like this my mother
would have made buttermilk.

It is afternoon now – always
afternoon when I return –

My mother must be
in the kitchen now — making tea —
boiling milk — the whole house
    smelling of buffalo milk —
and fresh tea —

Soon, my father will walk past me
        on his way home —
He with his long stride,
    his fast pace —
mosquitoes keep away from him —
bats fear him — When he looks at trees
does he still think about cholera?

Red ants shudder against earthworms.

But no one has died yet —
        no one is sick.

My brother is hiding somewhere.
I think he's behind the house —
On days like this we played
        hide and seek —

Although I know
    other people live here now —
Although it is my daughter
who is eleven,
    almost twelve now —
        today, I am alone —

I am ten, barely ten:
        still far enough away
from getting my period,
far away from womanhood —   far
away from ever leaving this garden.

Don't speak to me of exile.
Don't question my memory.

How can you understand
        the souls of brain cells?

How can you understand
            coefficients
        you have never even lived?

Only the palm tree mocks me –
reminds me of Time –
The palm tree that was never
        there before – Today
it stands huge and awkward –
        a clumsy mistake planted
in a strange place –
            the wrong place –
        It breaks the open circle
of grass where we used to run –

Telemann's Frogs

for Pearse Hutchinson

Reling.
Die Relinge, he called them.
Or perhaps, *Möhmlein, Rühling, Roeling* –

Sumpffrosch, Teichfrosch, Krotten –
        it is written,
Wasserfrosch und Wassereidechse.

They are yellow-gold,
        almost reddish yellow,
and their bellies
        are speckled black.

And for you, Pearse, I add:
        schwarz geschekigt.

Telemann's frogs.
They are here –
        have you noticed
how they appear
after the water music?
They are elegant, so elegant,
as if they were gods in disguise,
or a gathering of enchanted princes.

*

One summer
I listened to Telemann
as if he were a dear friend,
as if I expected him to come over
        for dinner any day.

I can still see myself,
I can see *her,*
the young woman I used to be.

Afternoon tea
with *Hamburger Ebb' und Fluth.*
A foreign woman in a foreign country,
in love with strangeness, otherness.
She heard a language
in which she could become
someone else — a third person, a fourth person —
Who is more alien?

Hamburger Ebb' und Fluth.

Must there be an ocean nearby,
a sea gulled breeze from the North Sea?

Or will the trams in Bremen do?
The trams she watched
from huge, arched windows
                beside her chair —
trams sliding through the rain
        on Ostertorsteinweg,
that old road leading to Hamburg —

To live on a street with such a name
        required Telemann.

But the trams interrupted
with their sudden rush of speed,
    their metal and glass
noise cutting through
    an endless screen of rain.

So she lifted her eyes from the page
she was reading in your book —
then listened again
            to the overture,
                again to the flutes,
the violins — she listened again
        even more acutely
before she returned
    to your world.

★

Pearse, that summer I read
your poems for the first time –
Entered your Dublin, your Barcelona.
Your 1950s echoing with Gaelic,
    with Castilian and Catalan –

That summer I kept
    returning to your words.
And always, in the background:
Thetis sleeping, Thetis awakening,
Neptune in love – *Ebb' und Fluth,*
Ebb' und Fluth, Neptune in love –

And always, love.
Always, the aching pull of it –
An unknown creature grasping the soul.

Buddha's Lost Mother

The mask
the mask-maker didn't want to sell
ended up with you –
          a favour, a gift
you brought back from Korea.

A mask so human,
          a laughing shaman –

Smooth pale wood,
          heavy and firm –

Face of an old man,
               his long hair tied up
into a loose knot
on top of his head –

Face of an old man, who could be
          an old woman in reality.

An old woman in hiding –

Buddha's lost mother.

Anonymous would have looked like this,
          I'm certain.

But will she feel at home
               over here, on our wall
          with the crocodile
mouth from Indonesia, a deep red mask
with whom she probably has nothing in common.
     Will she mind
the pretending-to-sleep masks from Nigeria?

The scent of green ginger
                    fills my kitchen.

Every day her laughter
          grows more pungent.

Gale Force Winds

January –
    Gale force winds
and the North Sea feels even closer.

Someone will drown today.
Someone will need
        to be rescued.

This winter sun has peeled back
our sky to a feverish, blinding blue.

I'm refilling jars with spices.
     As I release them,
   as I pour them from paper into glass,
I recall my mother's instructions,
    her recipes, her ginger cures
        for almost every ailment.

Our house with its spine of thirty-nine steps:
        a steep, winding mountain trail –
  our house from cellar to attic
smells of turmeric and coriander,
cumin, cinnamon, cardamom –
but most of all, there's the fragrance
        of red chilli.

Upstairs, my daughter's budgies cry out –
sun struck, wild,
    how these parakeets squawk and screech.

All morning
    our house shudders –
  groans as if in pain –   sighs against the wind.
Outside, the straightest, tallest birch tree
sways back and forth, almost bowing down
to our house. The tree moans, creaks
as if in answer to our windows.

When I close my eyes,
suddenly coriander
        and cinnamon are stronger –
When I close my eyes
I feel as if I'm on a ship
        already far out at sea.
I could be anywhere:
        on the Indian Ocean,
in the South Pacific –

Suddenly, I feel as if our house could be a ship, as if
that were the greatest desire of our house:
        to become a ship.
While the birch tree keeps calling, calling,
        in its strained, tortured speech
    as if it wanted to move indoors
        and become our mast, and steady
our house against the wind, and help our house to sail out
        and fulfil itself, for surely today
it would find the North Sea
        just around the corner –

While upstairs, two parakeets fly
        in circles, feathers lit by the sun,
            as if they knew all along,
    as if they knew everything
        about the need for such a journey –

Living with Stones

It's another age –
The continents have rejoined each other,
they've moved close together
          as tightly as they can,
     clasping each other like lost children.

And then, once again,
               they've split apart
bursting out into new formations.

They keep sliding, unable
to decide where they want to be.

Oceans that had never touched,
     suddenly meet –
Waves roaring at each other, stones
colliding, not knowing
     which shore they belong to.

We've collected those stones.

At first, they merely slept
               in our garden,
hibernated on the wooden floors
          in our house.

Of course, they continued breathing.

And then, one day,
their souls began echoing sounds
          from trees and ferns,
and from cats that would never go near the sea.

Now I see them everywhere:
               on our windowsills, bookshelves –
They've even taken over my desk.

How do they feel,
   living with strangers?

A huge, bluish grey stone from the Baltic,
      with patches of milky white,
lies snug against
      Connecticut granite.

Driftwood and sand dollars,
and the small, smooth black stones
      from the Pacific
surround shell encrusted chunks,
those creamy yellow fossils
         from Spain's Atlantic cliffs.

Fragments, secret fragments
            from the Indian Ocean –
Remember, remember:
      as we stepped out of the water
in Durban, white butterflies
         encircled us –   followed us –

 An inconspicuous stone
         from the Yellow Sea –

Startling white coral
         from the Strait of Makassar –

Somehow
      they've learned to live with us.

These nights they argue with the moon,
      challenge the stars –

These nights they've started to navigate
the mood of our silence,
      the rush of our sleep –

Piece Caprice

for Bob Zieff, the composer

Piece Caprice —
How bamboo grows
sheltering a stone Buddha.

Morning prayers linger in the air —
Goldfish awaken the pond's surface.

Whose garden have I entered?
Whose world do I walk in?
            Could it also be mine?

★

Piece Caprice —
Chet Baker's trumpet
fills my room,
    Paris spills out with your tune,
Bob, and 1955 begins again —   Oh yes,
there's a balcony —   Oleander,
roses, wild jasmine —
Terracotta soaks up
        excess water —

'But have you heard
        the version with violin?'
You ask.
'See how a violin changes the mood —
Does Dick Wetmore
come closer to you?'

★

Piece Caprice —   What
is the meaning of so much colour,
of all this blue?

You, blue-footed boobies, with your bright
turquoise dance –   Tell me
why blue? Must blue always enchant?

★

Piece Caprice –
You, blue-tongued lizards
          of Australia,
have you swallowed indigo?
What makes you think
your huge blue tongues
will frighten me? Why blue?

★

Piece Caprice –
And then, there was Vajradhara.
In the story I was told:

All the blue from the skies,
and the blue from the seas,
yes, the most intense blue from eternity
lives within this Buddha's skin.

This Buddha, Vajradhara.
He smiles.
For even his tiniest hairs are dark blue,
and even his meditation is blue.

His face, the colour of a morning glory:
          blue streaked with white,
                    luminous
with water and sun –

Tibetan lapis lazuli blue,
                    Chinese white –

Brushstrokes learnt in Kashmir,
          Nepalese shadows –

There's a strong wind
              from somewhere –
it must be a celestial wind.

And then, Tibetan light:
              intense and pure,
and strangely gentle.

 A light
    I wish existed
         within my soul.

                    ★

Now look again
  at this Buddha, Vajradhara:
such strength
       in his slender fingers –
such grace, such power
       in his lithe form –

As if the artist had meant
to create a leopard,
         or a deer –
but at the last moment
had formed his lines
into the shape of a man.

He sits with his head inclined,
his waist slightly bent
         as if he were listening,
just listening and swaying,
         almost dancing
   to a music we cannot hear.

All his garments swirling,
         encircling him
in pale rose red and lavender,
pink, pink, and malachite green,
         pale green –

How his scarves flutter
in these mountaintop winds.

★

Piece Caprice –
Whose world do I walk in?
Whose world
will I understand?

Whose Ghost Is This?

It is a face unknown to her –

A man, never seen before –
    at least, not by her.

Narcissus would have followed
him, instead of his own reflection
     in that lake.

More patient than Apollo,
    more eloquent than Orpheus –

Imagine
  all the colours of the sea
reflected in his eyes,
and his eyes ever changing with the light.

And the light, ever shifting
    through the sea,
and through the sky –

Yet, the sea is far away –

Whose ghost is this, returning?

Who is it that enters unbidden?

Will she touch his face?
Will his hair smell of the sea?
And his skin, will it taste of salt?

And then – ?

Too simple to say
it's the beginning of desire,
the beginning of beauty
    tightening within her being.

But what else?

He dares to speak to her,
and she dares to answer back –

He describes a garden,
he speaks of flamingos –

He suggests a departure
for the truly unknown.

And is she brave enough?

Hyacinths

Is that a girl or a boy,
that long-haired child
who runs across your fields?

You shrug, don't answer,
but show me hyacinths –

Hyacinths:
    bluish violet,
dark lavender ones –
    Thick fleshy stems
rubbery green bulbs
    squeak against each other
as you arrange them in water –
You choose a clear glass vase
    so we can watch
the mud swirling out,
the green becoming greener –
Those stems soon swollen
        with water –

Jasmine Tastes Bitter

What happened to them?

Where are they now,
      the ten Sibyls
    Augustinus sought
and knew and listened to?

All his muses silenced so quickly –

Jasmine tastes bitter,
   richly bitter
after so much sun –
  And look, the bees have returned.

Everyone has forgotten
how to speak with a Sibyl,
forgotten what gifts
    she might like –

Suji

A naming ceremony

He said:
One syllable is not enough.
And three syllables are far too many.
But *Suji* sounds just right.

So Suji remained.

Half English, half Hindi, half joking –

Isn't that what you wanted?
Pasta for the rest of your life?
    And red wine?

Suji   semolina   slippery

    leaves of basil awaken your tongue.

Monkey Woman

Your theories cannot
           explain her life.
How will you explain the monkey from Durban,
the one who lives in her kitchen?
His stance, almost human,
his limbs, smooth tropical wood,
hands cupped around his mouth
as if he were calling out to Pinocchio.

Your theories cannot explain her life.

Real monkeys have taken up
           all the space in her mind.
They are loud, hungry. There's the sound
           of rustling branches, the smell
of leaves being torn. This is exile, she says,
when you don't know where
           to keep the monkeys.

Now she waits
           for the year of the monkey.
Now she touches
           the jade-green smile
of a broad-headed monkey,
pale green porcelain,
           mother and child
bought from a Korean man in New York City.
Mother and child match
a tiny monkey
           bought in Korea,
a tiny, open-mouthed monkey,
crying O, O, O...
as if he had just bitten on a piece of ginger.

Pale green porcelain, the glaze
reflects a German sky, clouds rushing through
such wet blueness. The glaze even turns
           shadows translucent.

She thinks they speak to her
and she tries to understand them.
'Oh, where are you going?'
          She hears them say.
Her fingers memorise the mother's smile.

While on the other side of the room,
cast-iron monkeys from Andalusia
are wary, inscrutable. She thinks
          they guard her soul.

Lightning

Lightning –   a snake's tongue –
Your green life charred black and white.
Who can speak of it?

In the End

In the end one might go away
and speak to the snakes
        on Medusa's head.

Who knows what secrets they hoard.

The trick is to remain calm,
to begin with philosophical questions:

Ask them why the hero
sings alto, always –
        why the hero's voice
never goes deeper than a tenor.

Alto that sings of lilies –
tenor resilient as a green vine –

Ask them why
the hero has a woman's voice.

We were told
    the snakes are often hungry,
unreachable – for they make Medusa swim
       far out into the sea.

We were told the snakes are blind,
    told that they're tired of being stuck
        on Medusa's bruised head.
    And now they refuse to speak.

But who has ever bothered
      to listen to their story?

Korean Angel

Dieser Engel soll dein Haus beschützen. Ria Eïng

You bring me another angel.

She does not terrify. She's not fierce.
She's not even angry. Nor is she sullen.
There's nothing spiky about her.

How will she guard my house?

For this is the angel of gentleness –
                    water and light
sliding across stones. This is the angel
        of your strength.

She's Korean, I can tell
                    she's your secret.

Her face is open.
You've scooped it out into openness:
        into the beginning
    of something.

A faceless face.
            It remains.

A lidless, eyeless space.

Shall I call it a socket?

But there is clarity.

I can imagine a face
            hidden by shadows
and yet illuminated
            by the soft sheen
        of pearls through fog.

But it remains a faceless face.

And yet, this space
could be a wooden well
for a doll – it could become
a ring for your thumb –
but it's far too large, alas,
some would say, *if only, if only...*

Her face is open:
      a hole through her brain,
a hole through the sky –
there's a membrane
in the back of her mind, sheer silk
blossoming and blossoming
                with light.

Or is it a halo?

Soul-catcher?

Empty space waiting for someone's soul?

Off-white on almost white, dreaming of?
What? Striving for? What?
Truthful white? What's genuine?

What do you mean?

White sand, fine-grained white sand
        all the way down to the horizon –
Off-white colours of raw silk –

Raw silk you play with,
twisting it around your wrists, your shoulders –

White butterflies skimming across pale straw.

Sun bleached yellows.

Uncooked rice and sea salt in your hands.

How did you make her live?

Look, the instructions are in Korean:
a firm script, striding in black
at such precise right angles.

Her dress is a secret code, billowing
          with radio stories, resilient
rice paper rustling
          with radio static
                    she calls magic.

Six crows give up
          but a blackbird stays.

We speak of acupuncture,
we speak of next winter –
When shall we meet again?

You point at the wedge of wall
between two windows, where light
floods in, smelling of birch trees –
light washes in like a silent tidal wave –

Midsummer northern European light –
It is endless, brighter than eternity.

That's where we place the angel,
on a new nail –
                    soul-catcher halo
     breathing in all the light
as we speak of acupuncture –

kikku no sekku

Red chrysanthemums
give me five suns in the sky.
The bees are confused.

★

White chrysanthemums
dream of white swans with hot blood.
white clouds bring no rain.

★

Orange petals smell
sharper – turmeric hunger
burns a dragon's tongue.

★

It's virus weather.
Blossoming chrysanthemums
will cool your fever.

★

Harvest moon yellow,
chrysanthemum silk yellow –
who stole from whom?

★

A bee sleeps between
wet chrysanthemum petals –
bereft and queenless.

★

Green shadows grow long –
Chrysanthemums yearn for birds –
I pour tea for you.

Green tea steeps again –
Chrysanthemum buds open –
newborn in autumn.

★

What fragrance is this?
Yellow chrysanthemums breathe,
crave a tiger's voice.

★

Fat spiders climb up
white spider chrysanthemums –
sticky white rice steams.

★

Harvest-moon-faced, this
golden chrysanthemum sways –
an infant cries out.

★

Star within star within
star unfolds, white petals tinged
green – do your eyes ever close?

★

Lightning – she lingers –
a chrysanthemum bows down.
Hair tangled with bees.

★

Birds hover over
such deep red chrysanthemums.
The bees are fearless.

★

Orange, bronze, violet –
these petals never clash.
Will you walk with me?

III

Sad Walk

Four Poems: Paula Becker Speaks

Black Sails

Paula Becker to Rainer Maria Rilke, September 1900. Worpswede

Black sails: greased and tarred –

Black sails of boats laden with turf –

They glide down the river –
I see them sliding through
             trees –   Black sails
     between sunlit patches
        of birch bark –

Every day the light pulls me
             out further – somewhere
further outside of myself –

Today I think these boats
     come out of hell –
dripping with black blood
     from the moors –
dragging out
        the smell of marshlands,
of rotting leaves –

You tell me
     we must learn
how to welcome back
the dead – they are always there, you say,
and we must learn to live with them –

Even now, some days
     they pull out corpses
             from the bog –
Dead bodies
from Roman times – their tired wrinkles
        seem to sweat –

Later
we bury them in the churchyard –

Is that a true way
    of welcoming?

Perhaps the turf I burn
once covered the face of a woman –
This turf, grown thick
    and rich against her skin –

A woman
who might have looked like me –

Perhaps tonight
I will burn bits of her hair
without truly knowing that I do –

Hair that might have been
    as long as mine –

Now lost, peat entangled,
peat ensnared –   prickly
with moss and rough seeds –

A married woman
   who took a lover –

You told me how
   they punished her:

Face down, naked
  they made her lie
down on the moor,
   in the wettest part of the bogland –
all the tender parts of her body
   tightening against the coldness –
all her pores curled and puckered
    in anguish –

Then,
the farmhands stepped on her –
the largest men walked over her
        stamping her into the mud –

The stickiness taking her in –

How the air must have hummed
                seething around her –
Even the mud
                seething with her soul –

This brownish black Worpswede mud –
how strong, how dark
        it must have been
    a thousand years ago – The stickiness
taking her in –
        A glistening being –
Did she still think
        it was Mother Earth?

Her nose, mouth, ears
stuffed shut with spongy loam –

They stamped on her
        until she was deep enough –
Their own legs thick with –   with –

You say, betrayal
        is too simple a word –
Too convenient
    to call it adultery –

You tell me even now
you can see her face –
        hear what she felt
    centuries ago:
fear, disgust, anger –
her distorted face stays with you –

Then, stays with me
as if she were a black rose
you had pressed for me –
as if I must keep her
for you –
as if I have no choice –

You Kissed My Eyelids

Paula Becker to Rainer Maria Rilke, March 1902. Worpswede

Last year
you kissed my eyelids –
or was it an accident – your lips
brushing against my face?
You, the gentlest man who
ever touched me –

And then we spoke of Death –
And then we were silent.
That's when I knew I loved you.
I loved you because of the silence –
because I could be silent
with you –

*

One day in Berlin
Clara entered our room
and I knew
you were lovers.
It was the way you looked up,
the way she stepped towards you –
Your bodies fulfilled yet aching –
And suddenly I was far away –
I could not breathe.

And I am still far away –

Because you could not have me
you took Clara —
Clara, whom I love
the most —   And now, what
have you done to her?
How could you
          change her so much?
Why must you
          make her into your echo?

Sometimes
I think you do it
     to spite me
to punish me.

Even you are not yourself anymore.

Yes, I am angry at you,
               at Clara —

But most of all, angry
          at myself —

Colours freeze in my mind.
All my greens and browns
          are dying —

My blues and yellows
          suffocate me.

If only I had been free enough,
strong enough to love you back —

I was ignorant —
          full of illusions.

Otto is a façade.

I miss Clara's hands,
her fingers in my hair.

And your kisses, Rainer –
That's what I crave:
Your kisses from those first days
when you were pure
        and truly yourself
in my atelier –
beyond all poses and pretensions –

But I don't understand love –

All morning I listened
    to the birds
growing louder and louder
    and in between
the rain falling – now stopping,
now starting again in a rush –
All morning I waited for Clara.
I thought she might come to see me,
to surprise me the way she used to.
It was a feeling I had.
    Clara *must*
come by today, I thought –
A teasing premonition –
        completely false –
while birdcalls interrupted
    my mind all morning –
and I remembered your kisses
Rainer –   your hands –

Elsbeth

Paula Becker to Clara Westhoff, July 1902

Elsbeth:
    tall as a foxglove stalk –

Elsbeth: lost within her song –

She walks away
    and the foxglove bends
away from her –

Ripe pink thimbles
    Elsbeth ignores –

Back to back they move apart –

She must sing a song.

Does she remember
    her dead mother?

She must have hens
that cluck and lay brown eggs –

She must have blue mist
    falling over the grass –

And her white dress
    cannot be too white –
It must have blue dots.

Elsbeth is far away
    deep inside her song –

and she lets me follow –

Runic

Paula Becker to Clara Westhoff, 1905

I want to paint runic faces.

They must be runic – filled
    with my own
    loneliness –

Simple geometry, you say —
and yet, it's impossible
        to know
the angles I need, the colours —

I know
        strength,
I know shadow —

And pressure, height, breadth —

    I can measure eyes —

But how shall I find my own
                runic core?

Sometimes there's a noise
rising up within me —
as if the distant thunder
lives inside me — and is not distant —

And I hear all the ancient,
        antique mouths
            from the Louvre
speaking — softly at first,
a gentle whispering — But some days
they grow loud, anxious,
            impatient —

The Imagination

in response to a painting by William Johnstone

Three horizontal brushstrokes
and the imagination is delighted.

Land and sea and sky
all grey –   black grey, white grey –
silk unravelling into translucent
                    watery grey.

There's texture:
waves and stones and clouds –

Three horizontal brushstrokes –

The imagination believes
it's four in the morning,
it's summer –   and we're on the shore
by the open Pacific.
Still too early to know
more, but the fog will lift
the day will be blue.

Three horizontal brushstrokes –

The silence in a breath not taken
before green tea is poured.

Water in a brush
controlled with a flick of the wrist.

One of those movements:
incidental to all appearances –
       deceptive, unconscious,
and yet attainable
only after sixty,
maybe seventy years of painting.

Three horizontal brushstrokes –

She Slipped Through the Suez Canal

She slipped through the Suez Canal
on a steamer that left Southampton,
    a steamer destined for Bombay.

And years later,
it felt like someone else's life.

She slipped through the Suez Canal –

And then it was a song she liked to sing,
    a memory she liked to open,
where she was *she.*

A steamer destined for Bombay –

'Returning home', it was called back then
    in 1964 –   not visiting but returning.

Home was always far away.

Being seven she didn't understand
the sudden silence after dinner –
    the nervousness on board,
why no one spoke to children anymore.

It was a night crossing.
Slow, tense –   with everyone listening
    to the steamer's noise
and a jerking, halting movement –
    stops and starts
    that kept her awake.

But she knew the stars were out
offering their help. She had seen the moon,
and she was certain there were night birds
somewhere –   calling, calling – she was certain
    she had heard them crying all night –

And then, there was the hoopoe
    in the Gulf of Aden –
but now she's jumping ahead.

She slipped through the Suez Canal –

And years later, as she gave birth,
she remembered that journey –

The Light that Unfetters the Soul

*Am I naive, Vanessa, to expect that in this country, I will see, in a miracu-
lous moment, the light that unfetters the soul and gives it the wings to fly like
a free bird, unencumbered by feelings of guilt or contrition? Will such a
moment ever come?*

Aharon Megged

Will such a moment ever come?
And is this light available
only in one country, in one place?

Or could it be almost anywhere?
So each soul must find its own light,
　　　　its own geography –

And where does one begin?
How does one choose a country,
a season, a form of light?

And look: the olives ripen, the lizards stretch

for Eleanor Wilner

And look: the olives ripen,
these fruits the shape of human eyes,
these little stones – thousands hang on trees.
They're resistant to the wind; dull green, blind.
Yet their hard skins grow warm as spring changes into summer,
as wildflowers take over;
everywhere *the lizards stretch,*
the thin slivers of their bodies licked by sun,
pale browns and greens and black stripes glisten.

She leans back against a tree, holds her breath
for a few seconds, keeps the lizards in her gaze.
She stretches in the sun; the smell of rosemary
mingles with the smell of sea; in the distance
children call out to each other. The infant
in the basket beside her stirs; she touches him
before he makes a sound. The lizards
in her gaze, she leans back again.
Her book lies open, almost forgotten.
Her scribbled notes resemble the curling stems of vines
and lizards' feet. She strokes the infant's legs,
dares not touch his face, dares not awaken him
before he's hungry for her milk. The smell of sea
mingles with the smell of goat cheese and olives,
and the smell of rosemary. The lizards are not afraid.
Today they won't dart away. They want to live
beside her silence, her milky solitude that grows
across the fields; they want to be close
to her quietness, full of the infant's sleep.

Three Poems from South Korea

Bamboo in Gyeongju

Bamboo in Gyeongju –
   bamboo in Gyeongju –

One wants to say it over and over again –
   oo, oh, oo –   *oo, oh, oo*

And the bamboo in Gyeongju
     is tall and lush and wild
beside small grassy hills,
  hills that are actually tombs.

Here, the earth has the silhouette
   of a sleeping woman –

Let's hope she's sleeping,
    sleeping and not sick
       or poisoned or dead –

Long ago, when the tiger still smoked
       with the hare,
  one could say she slept soundly and deeply.
She slept a sleep that refreshed her
   profoundly –   Long ago,
when the tiger still smoked with the hare –

Still, the bamboo in Gyeongju
     grows tall
and every stone lives,
   and I want to believe
  that soon,
the giant stone turtle will move –

King Munmu

Some say his ashes
   have been eaten by the sea.
Others believe they lie cradled
   within a beautiful urn
still intact, somewhere
   at the bottom, beneath a rock –

But we know
King Munmu's soul lives underwater
   within the body of a dragon.

Nights he spits out stones –
gems for the girls, such blues and greens –

Girls who walk along the beach
   slowly, deliberately –
lipsticked precisely,
   long-skirted and lean –
they share orchid-coloured intimacies –

Hands balancing stones,
they walk through seaweed –

The air smells of algae, of dried fish –

Old women have come here
   to pray, to meditate –
they're waiting for the dragon,
   especially his tail,
they feel so sure of seeing –

They long to watch it lash the waves,
   slap the sea to attention –
as if that would offer protection,
   as if it would bring back the dead –

They sit motionless, listening –
while the dragon dives deeper,

his tail gliding down
as he slips further away from the shore –

Because of the Moon

Gyeongju, 2007

Because of the moon,
the fullness, the gold,
we step outside –

Because of the moon, because
of the movement of the clouds,
we go to the pond
and keep walking around it –

Because of the moon
we listen to frogs –

Because of the moon
we still feel the young monk's song,
yes, we feel his deep voice,
his words from this morning
within our bones,
his athletic devotion, the richness
of his prayers this evening –
all this we cling to, all this
still echoes within us
even as we listen to the frogs –

Because of the moon
we follow narrow paths
further and further into the thicket –

Because of the moon
when we close our eyes
we still see the face
of a bodhisattva
carved so faintly in the rock

that one can see it only
from a certain distance, a certain angle —

Because of the moon
    we return to the pond,
        oddly shaped, huge —
and watch how moonlight snags on bamboo,
    how shadows slide, black and sheer,
        nudging greenness —

Because of the moon
    we stay outside —

Finding India in Unexpected Places

for Martin and Connie Mooij

A street in Bath,
     a bus in Medellín,
a gesture in Gyeongju –

A yellow fragrance in Oaxaca,
     Oleanders
          on the isle of Skopelos –

Memories distort geography.

But how did the Mayas
     learn about elephants,
about Ganesh, and the precise shape
          of his ears?

Six Entries from a Witch's Diary

for Robin Skelton

i

Japanese maple:
the sun bleeds through its young leaves.
A soldier walks by —
Athletes cry out, so alert —
They keep on playing war games.

ii

Even the doctor
left the bat in her bedroom
all day — Did it sleep?
Waiting for darkness, somehow
she will help it find its way.

iii

Flying fox, it's you
I fear, as mosquitoes swarm at dusk,
and tamarinds snap
in sudden gusts of wind —   how long
will you stay in our garden?

iv

Umbrian lizard
glistens: black-streaked green jewel —
but the tail trembles,
and blood shines pink through its skin.
How your loud shoes change the tune.

v

A chameleon sways
rocking back and forth with each step –
We're north of Durban.
Five poets climb out of a jeep
and wait for this dancer to pass –

vi

Filigreed lace feet
clinging to a whitewashed wall –
'Don't write only about lizards!'
my daughter says. Little does she know
my life is lizards –

Zinzirritta

It's easy to love swallows.
I watch them as they circle
        high above the rooftops –
now swooping down, now darting up, zipping by faster
        and faster –   my dolphins of the air
with their high-pitched squealing, squeaking song –
how they swerve between these old, red-roofed houses,
        north German houses, not far from the sea.

Such energetic feeding lasts
        the whole evening,
as if they wanted to catch
        every insect before the bats emerge.

It's the bats I'm waiting for,
        trying to understand –

As a girl, in Poona, I remember
running away from them, afraid
they would bite off my ears,
or worse, that they would manage to squeeze
themselves deep inside my inner ears, my head –
        two at a time –

                    ★

Flying rodents, flying foxes –
I've been collecting the roots of their names,
        their photographs –

Here in Lübeck, in Ravenna,
        they are tiny, harmless –

Pipistrello
        I like to call them –
and *zinzirritta*,
            mesmerising *zinzirritta* –

What sound contains their essence?
Their true nature?

Flittermouse, flickermouse, flindermouse
flintymouse, *Fledermaus* –

Their young ones fly a crooked loop –
lopsided stop and go –
black leaves falling, falling –   but then rising up
suddenly, as if caught by the wind –

Hreremus, leather flapper,
flapper, shaker –

★

Leather flapper, your wings tremble –

Your skin: shiny, moist,
part hairless, part velvet –
your thin silk just as thin as ours.

Incessant

Incessant, unearthly speech
from creatures so close to the earth –

These night crickets in Caracas –

Mechanical birds, I thought at first,
computer *sirena* voices –

How I turn and turn
        trying to follow them.

How they interpret and reinterpret Erik Satie –

And they must know Philip Glass –

Precise, constant,
    they take over –
even my private night.

Unexpected Blackness

Caracas, July 2005

Because I had never seen a black squirrel
I thought it was the blackest thing on earth.

Blacker than the blackest Labrador,

blacker than the blackest face of a langur,

blacker than Kazuko Shiraishi's hair
                which the squirrel appraised
in its own fashion.

Never mind obsidian,
        let alone a raven.

Don't think of the deepest well
on a moonless, starless night.

Forget coal, forget oil.
This squirrel was blacker
than the blackest core within our earth.

And what did we do,
        Kazuko and I?

We stood there wondering
        'What next?'

Would this squirrel dare
        to let go
of the bark on its tree
and leap over
        across Simón Bolívar's shoulders?

Or was it tame enough to show respect?

We stood there learning this squirrel by heart,
following its well-fed, glossy movements –

We stood there learning this blackness by heart,
a blackness pulsing through
                    sun slashed trees,
    rippling with so much light,
        we felt we must begin again,
    alter our journey, prolong our silence,
                relearn our selves –

Sad Walk

for Bob Zieff – *remembering our endless conversations*

Who would have thought
     a sad walk
would lead to *pozole*?

        ★

I could take this story
     almost anywhere –

        ★

Let Time be a wide, tight spiral –
so Kierkegaard could still
be walking down the streets
of Copenhagen –   how adept he is
     at leaping over
puddles –   It's the sort of day when windows
must be opened –   and in the distance
     a man can be heard singing,
while someone nearby
     is tuning a piano –
It's the sort of day when children get lost.

        ★

We speak of Kierkegaard
as we follow the movements
     in a Chinese sculpture –
glistening porcelain
blossoming with lotuses,
     Buddhas
and Barbie doll heads.

        ★

Only in spring does the year feel new.
Only in spring do we begin
              to crave lemons and hyacinths –
while girls swirl by in skirts
            with lime green pleats.

                    ★

It's a young man's sadness
                  I hear –
a young man's sadness
filled with sea air –

                    ★

Is Time within you,
or is it outside?

                    ★

I want the Atlantic Ocean
to be a part of my garden.

                    ★

I want to listen to violins
as I step in the water.

IV

Solo Piano

Radishes

Somewhere
the Great Chain of Being continues unfolding
        as I chop radishes,
as I chop off
        their tough, scraggly tails,
it's mice I'm thinking of, hundreds of mice
and all their tails –
        and the largest vein
in the centre of each tail –
Not large at all
but a pulsing filament –
        Fine, so fine –
And how one day, I searched for that vein
        in a hundred tails –
simply to inject each one with a virus:
        encephalitis –
Whose child will be spared?
        Whose life?

Jane Eyre in the Lab

Don't you remember?
It was the Indian woman, Kamal,
    who brought her in,
who brought Jane Eyre
all the way down to Pathology,
      our almost secret lab
hidden in the basement
         of this hospital.

It was October in Baltimore, a day
      when the wind
wanted to swallow everything.

It was the sort of day that made our boss,
    Dr Arnold, seek out Mozart.

It was the week the surgeons had left
for their convention. It was a week without tumours,
    a week without mastectomies.

Dr Arnold remained in his office,
    uninterrupted,
        with Mozart.
He turned the volume up higher and higher
as if that would eradicate cancer.

After three days
Jane Eyre felt at home in our lab.
She preferred to sit by the radio.
She was not disturbed
    by the fluorescent lights
that flickered and hummed and buzzed
like swarms of desperate insects.
And the smell of hydrochloric acid
    was never unbearable to her.

We had plenty of time
to get reacquainted with Jane.

But she was quiet, reluctant to speak,
even as she watched us endlessly.

And yet, she persisted in asking questions.
How can you trust ——? A machine?
A surgeon? A man? What will happen
to those women waiting
        in their beds upstairs?
Why do we never see them?

Kamal remembers
that day she slid the book
        out of her bag.
A hardback library edition,
dark evergreen embossed
with gold. Kamal remembers
her hands stroking the pages,
how she started reading:

There was no possibility of taking a walk that day.

Oh, to be in England, Kamal thought,
        and to feel
    a rain so penetrating...
She wanted to weave her own pain
        with fierce weather.

So Kamal, 24 years old and newly bereft,
        sat by the microscope
and took Jane's sorrow into herself.

Sometimes, Dr Arnold walked in
and watched Kamal and nodded.
'Good, you took my advice.
You might as well read,' he would say,
'there's nothing else to do.'

And Kamal felt she was the dearest reader
        of Jane Eyre's tale.
She could almost hear Jane say:

But this is not to be a regular autobiography.

I longed to go where there was life and movement.

Sometimes, Kamal grew restless.
     She paced up and down
        airless corridors.
She lingered outside
     Dr Arnold's door,
       just to hear the violins.

And one day, Jane smiled
to herself and walked up to Irena,
yes, Irena, from Moscow,
     a scientist who worried
about her twelve-year-old daughter's
     desire for high heels.
Hello, Jane said to Irena,
I wonder, she almost stammered,
     would you tell me how –
would you teach me some Russian?

Nights, Kamal wrote long letters
     to her sister in London.

'Oh, to be in England, in autumn.
Lucky you.' She wrote
and felt even closer to Jane.

Jane, I will not marry him,
   I cannot. Never.

Kamal imagines saying.

Come with me, Jane. Stay with me.
I am not very tranquil in my mind.

Kamal wants to say.

Where shall we go? Jane asks,
     reading her mind –

And yet, Kamal could not
forget the list of tumours,
the list of names and dates of birth
of women she never saw.
All those women, upstairs,
            in their white beds
waiting for the surgeons to return.

Kamal remembers
how one day, that very week,
        on her way out
she heard screams
from the autopsy room.
Piercing, incessant screams
and then, *a curious laugh*
                or a sob
    from a room
        known for its silence.

While Dr Arnold remained
uninterrupted, in his office,
        with Mozart.

Nine Poems in Response to Lithographs by Paula Rego

Girl Reading at Window

While Jane reads
she becomes the sea and the sun
and all the reflections in the glass –

She becomes the window's clouds and flies and dust,
      the window's eggs and spiders, voice and soul,
the window's obedient daughter –

And now, the window
has a new story to tell.

Loving Bewick

Don't interrupt –

    When I'm loving Bewick
you don't exist for me.

I mean to absorb all this calcium –

I'm good at endurance,
swallowing pain, my angry words –

But this is love. Bewick gives me
new words to replace my rotten ones.

I want my teeth, my spine
      to be as strong as his beak.

Don't laugh. I'm going to learn
         how to do it.

I'm going to become Bewick –
      his words, his feathers,
I'm going to live with a bird's vision
        growing inside me.

Crumpled

Crumpled like a newspaper, Jane says.

Smudged, eroded.

Not just my skirts and undergarments –
    my soul too, all crumpled.

My face, my fingerprints –
    all crumpled.

What must I do
to make you understand?

Jane in a Chair with Monkey

Jane cannot look
    at her monkey –

Today she's Medusa
    and must ignore
everyone she loves.

Tomorrow,
it's her monkey's turn
    to play Medusa.

Jane's Back

There's nothing as sturdy
    and as straight
        as Jane's back.

Her spine is not the breakable kind.

And the nape of her neck
is a rectangular white slab.

It's the sort of back
  one can turn on the world.

And yet, the world won't notice.

Nonetheless, Jane's back will grow stronger.
It will grow into a door –   Solid oak
    it wants to be –   with a texture
everyone will want to touch,
a door, everyone will try to open.

Bertha

Bertha: all plum-stained,
ripe –   Bertha sits on the floor,
legs outstretched, arms about to be crossed
against her breasts –
    all plum-stained, love-stung, in full bloom, even
over-blossomed moist petals –
        and such a fragrance of magnolias –
all plum-stained, over-ripe, sly desire –
Bertha sulks
    a tropical rage
strong enough to rip coconuts off trees –
She's not insane,
    oh no –   She's just angry
at the man who left
before she had a chance
                to speak –

Biting

In reality
Bertha is young and shapely.

But no one knows this, no one
except the man who visits
her secretly, disguised as her brother.

Baa baa black sheep, take off your mask –

Look how he forces her –
makes her bite him
    again and again –

And then, one day he'll say
    she needs to be killed.

The Keeper

Whenever Jane sees
        Grace Poole with Bertha
she kneels and prays
        for her own mother.

Grace Poole and Bertha –
    Mother and child.
They demand worship,
        adoration.

But no matter how much Jane prays,
no matter how much her knees ache,
No one will ever
    give her a mother's love.

Lucky Bertha. She knows how to be
        irrational and mad.
It's just the right sort
    of insanity for Grace Poole.

Grace can hold Bertha down
        and still stare out the window
            at trees, clouds
and at the swallows who are
        searching for a new
            Thumbelina to rescue.

Come to Me

'Come to me.' He says,
raising his blind eyes
    to the light.

'Come to me!' He thinks
I'm a rabbit or a dog.
    But I'm not.

I'm a cat.
And I'll come and go
    as I please.

★

And then, Jane twists her mouth
    and gathers up her skirts.
Her hands, clenched tight –   poised
    as if to tear her clothes –

Four Poems in Response to Paintings by Paula Rego

The Cadet and his Sister

He wants to go.
It's getting late.
But she insists
on tying his shoelaces
the way she used to
when she was six
and he was three.

She threw down her gloves.
Her handbag popped open.
But he keeps looking
    at the road ahead,
at the trees.

And so in times of need
he'll remember the smell
of eucalyptus leaves.

If he comes back
from the war
he'll marry a girl
who's just like his sister.

If he dies
she'll name her son
after him.

She doesn't know
that soon enough
she'll have a baby, a boy
who'll be just like her brother.

A child only she
    will understand.

The Maids

Lice in your hair, Madame?
The maid asks.

No, she answers herself,
it's only a spider
       on the nape of your neck.
Here, let me take it off.

Thank you. Madame sighs.
Madame used to be Monsieur –
but then got tired of being a man.

She wanted more
pink and red in her life.

Stay with me Marie, will you –
Madame whispers to her maid.
And won't someone
take Louise to the zoo?

By 'someone' Madame means Teresa.
Teresa, that sly dreamer
who has broken so many plates.

But little Louise
with her golden hair
       already tangled,
doesn't want anyone to touch her.

Marie used to love Madame
when Madame was Monsieur.

And now she wishes
her true Madame
would come back.

The Soldier's Daughter

The soldier's daughter can pluck a goose
    faster than you can blink –

She loves it, sinking her hands
    into flesh still warm and supple
and ripping out the soft feathers
    damp with death –

The soldier's daughter is the one who's golden.
    Butter on those lips, peaches and cream –
Her thick legs gleam, all muscle.

Her grandmother can't sleep,
    prays for her night and day –
Prays for the goldenness to always stay.

The soldier's daughter sends her father to war.
It's to protect her,
    to defend her that he goes –

A small man with a big heart
    he knows that soon enough
his daughter will begin
    laying golden eggs –

The Policeman's Daughter

The policeman's daughter,
    with her tiny waist
    and her Greek nose,
is the most beautiful girl in town.

Trained to perfection,
    nothing can stain her.

Who else would dare
    to wear a white dress
while cleaning those boots?

The policeman's daughter
    is a natural queen –

And the policeman, that stubborn man,
    listens only to her.

She's the only one
who can tell him what to do –
        the only one
who can talk back to him.

She's the only one
who knows how to clean
        his boots.

Look, how easily
her arm slides into the boot
and how the boot goes all the way up
    stopping
        just inches below her shoulder.

Now her left fist is jammed in,
while her right fist bears down
            with the cloth –

Her energy looks like anger.
But she's not angry, she says.

The policeman's daughter
    is a natural queen –

Next year she'll marry
    the doctor's son –
A boy
  who wants a strong woman.

But tonight
  she'll stay at home –
    and keep the cat
from losing her virginity.

Portrait of a Young Man in his Study, Venice, 1528

in response to a painting by Lorenzo Lotto

It started with a lizard
  that fell out of his heart.
She lives on his desk now,
  amidst his letters.

And then his love returned
  his ring with a rose
the day before she died.

No wonder he's so pale,
he hasn't stepped out in weeks –
He cannot eat, cannot sleep –

They've taken his infant son
far away to another country –

He spends his nights reading –

But the lizard is good company
  and doesn't mind anything.

The Old Man Who Is Not

for Günter Kunert

The old man who is not
really that old, sits naked
with thirteen skulls
piled up high on his table.

Is it his desk or is it
a corner of his dining table?

Other people he knows
prefer to keep vases full of roses
and bowls overflowing with fruit –
especially apples. Other people prefer
    to keep apples nearby.

But his skulls stay –
even the grass-stained ones.
They need to speak to him.
Look, how impatient they are,
all talking at the same time,
interrupting each other.

The old man simply listens.

Flesh is still lavender, supple –
              even pink –
and today's light
is still golden – golden, filled with pollen,
thick with countless spores.
So golden, and yet it grows cold.
Love waits on the other side
of the room –   love bends to undress,
       she has undressed –
now she bends to pick up a fallen ribbon –
and now, turning away from the skulls
       love takes a deep breath –

Felice Beato Enters Sikander Bagh

Lucknow, March 1858

Felice Beato enters Sikander Bagh
    and rearranges the bones
in the courtyard of our palace,
        our battered, demolished palace –

Corpses that are actually skeletons –
He gives us the first photographs
    of human remains,
of a massacre he wants to recreate
       in an albumen silver print,
so you'll remember what happened
    in November 1857.
Two thousand men slaughtered
    and left to rot.
It was easy to find bones
    that were never buried –

How would you like our memories
    to be preserved?

Turn the page, the album leaf,
on which Beato's Sikander Bagh appears,
  and you'll see Martin Richard Gubbins,
Financial Commissioner, in the province of Oudh,
    narrator of mutinies, rebellions –
with his wife, Harriet Louisa,
    and daughter, Norah Louisa,
sitting with their tidy flowers,
waiting to be served tea, and more –

Yes, the very same Gubbins
    who killed himself in 1863.

The Smell of Lilacs

The smell of lilacs
    strengthened his nerves –

And he couldn't live without
    the smell of rotten apples –

This is where he sat and wrote
    Wilhelm Tell in six weeks –

And when he was tired
    he laid his head
        upon his desk
and took a nap.

He had two sons,
    Karl and Ernst.
And eight years after his death,
his widow, Charlotte, wrote this
to Ernst, the younger one:

*The desk has been newly stained
and stands under Karl's picture.
It's not meant to be used,
only by you – if you want.
It's comforting to me now
to see this desk –
it was painful before.*

★

We kept lilacs
    for the butterflies –
And every May, they blossomed.

And every May, she cut some branches
and brought them in the house.

★

These nights are so bright, we cannot sleep.
The moon keeps us awake
        and then, we wait for the nightingale.

These nights we listen
        to the animals outside,
their hunger taking over our lives.

★

Four bears live
 with five monkeys
        in a zoo.

Their keeper
wants them to fight
        but they don't.

Every day they can smell
human flesh burning, burning –
        It makes them sick.

The barbed wire,
on the other hand,
        feels important.

★

From the zoo
        one can see
the crematorium.

And over here
        we have the prisoners' latrines.
It's hard to keep everything clean.

Near the crematorium
        there's a cellar
with forty-eight hooks for the hangings.

And over here
    we have new barracks
for those who are good with their hands.

                    ★

And over here
between the bears and the monkeys
        and the crematorium —

between the prisoners' latrines
        and the cellar
with the forty-eight hooks for the hangings —

they brought Schiller's desk,
        to save it
from the bombings.

And then, they ordered their prisoners
        to make a copy of it.
But what did those prisoners think?

And can you imagine
    what they said
as they measured Schiller's desk?

                    ★

I imagine them silent,
    each lost in his own numbness.
Some of the workers were Norwegian.

Even Willy Werth, master craftsman,
    famous for his model ships —
Viking ships —   I imagine him silent.

Were they given apple wood?
    How far could they go?
Did they look back to the eighteenth century?

What sounds did they hear
    through the windows?
Could they hear the bears and the monkeys?

And if they spoke?
Did they speak of Schiller,
what they had learnt in school?

And were they free to speak their minds?
What would you have said, what would you have done
        to save your life?

★

18 October 1943.

At last, the copy
    of Schiller's desk is delivered.

A copy easily mistaken
    for the original.

A copy made in Buchenwald
        by prisoners.

And then, Schiller's own desk is stowed away
        in Nietzsche's house.

It is 1943.

    And I ask:

During these days
did anyone sit at Schiller's desk —
        at the copy of his desk?

And if so,
    then, what was done —
what was written there?

328 Mickle Boulevard, Camden, New Jersey

As we stood by your bed,
        I thought of whales –

And then our guide said:

'Looking at Walt here –
he wasn't too bad.
But for the last eight years
it was pretty hard.'

A few minutes later
we were reprimanded
    for tripping over
your green suede shoes.

Such beautiful shoes, deep moss green
        guarding your papers –

Piles and piles of your papers
all scattered just so – orderly disorder
watched over by your womanly, elegant shoes –
your tomboyish shoes –   delicate, clean and so new
        I couldn't believe
you ever wore them.

Your parents watched us
in every room – especially your mother.

Walt, your whole house is refurbished now –
    true to history – brighter than ever – windows
sparkle like wet eyes – Sepia lads
    suddenly dust free, vibrant again –

The buttery wallpaper reminded us of Italy,
        of vanilla ice cream in Florence.

Our guide allowed us to linger
at every corner, every threshold –
        his face intense with so much information
                he wanted to give and give –

The way he led us to your kitchen,
it was clear he lived with you.

Across from the stove
Mary Davis' fainting couch
gleamed sleek and smug
            and almost bristled –
lying stretched out
            with a large cat's
        languid, twitching alertness –

Then, we were led outdoors
                    into your garden –

November sun on a day in 2003 –
a cold wind ripping down ginkgo leaves
            slivers of milky gold
to match your fresh wallpaper –

We were told, you liked to walk out here,
we were told, Mary planted herbs –

Our guide knelt
beside a bed of Lambs' Ears.
'Take some of this,' he urged,
'take all of it – no one else will
and the winter will kill it.'

His hands poised to tear out
                swathes of leaves,
    roots and all –

We stopped him
and then stood mute –

Lambs' Ears – thick velvet
    a dull white-green
            paler than your shoes –

I took one leaf, still fragrant –
                faintly, lightly fragrant –
I took one leaf
                and left the rest for winter –

Abstractions

Harrisburg, Pennsylvania, 2004

The lost boys
of Sudan don't want to be called
'the lost boys'. They tell me this
over and over again. They want to speak
about the imagination, about ideas
and how what others call 'abstractions'
are not truly abstractions.
Ideas are real, but where
do they come from?
They ask me –
How do you get ideas for your imagination?
What do you mean,
the imagination is always there?
Where is it?
Ideas are animals and birds –
Ideas are birds
and the imagination
has to be everything:
the forest and the lake –
The imagination has to make them
        want to stay, the imagination
has to catch them.

                  *

Meanwhile, there's a lost girl
        who won't follow
'the lost boys' –

She'll sit beneath a tree
and let her fingers grow
            longer and longer –

Circling Over Medellín

Everyone gets off here
except us – we keep circling over Medellín,
        up and down the mountain.

Two hours have passed.
We sit boxed in glassy metal,
   metallic glass –
        sparkling new cable cars
where we've become the hosts.

Entire families pass through
showing us where they live now, where
        they used to live –
Where they were robbed,
    where someone was killed –
Here and there and here –

We look at their gardens,
    at their Medellín green –
at the brown of their earth
   and the shape of their homes –

What gardens? Over here?
    In these neighbourhoods?

Patches of dirt, a few flower-pots
between houses piled up on each other –
    shacks all along the mountain.
   Red brick everywhere:
the one beautiful, man-made colour
    stuck onto this land.

And yet, there are trees:
small, vibrant, upthrusting lushness –

And leafy bushes with their dark
    miraculous glistenings
to match any knife –

Clothes put out to dry,
arranged as if they were sending out signals
          to outer space —

Over there, a girl sits reading —
    And then,
          a woman steps out
on her terrace with the wash —

While on the other side,
               a boy out on his roof
    yet squeezed between walls,
          tries to fly a kite —
his house slanting, built at an angle
          on top of another house —

Oh, how that boy on his roof
          tries to fly a kite.

A House of Silence

Medellín 2005

This is where the murderer meets
    the sister of his victim,
the wife, the children –

This is where they work,
side by side, not knowing
    who the other is.

Not allowed to speak, we're told,
they must speak with their hands,
they must make something out of clay.

A deaf-mute boy is the first
to greet us, fatherless at seven –
He places his sculpture in our hands:

A man and a woman in a tight embrace –
their spines cut deep as rivers
in their perfect, passionate backs.

Other children create clay figures
who are born chopped up –   legs and arms,
torsos and even heads, lined up side by side.

The one I ask about is a pre-Columbian head
with a cradle on top, and a baby inside, intact –
I'm convinced it was made by an artist, a woman.

But no, I'm told, it was a boy of nine,
dead already, shot dead –   and no one to claim his work.
Take it, they say, take it. Nobody wants it.

Devibehn and Harilal in Pennsylvania

And for memory I had substituted inquiry. George Lamming

For weeks
they have been staring out my window –

Reduced to their black and white existence
on my bedside table,
    they stare at the colours
of a Pennsylvania October.

Colours they would have worn,
    I'm told –

Devibehn's sari, a delicate *chidri* –
She has wrapped herself
    in a thousand leaves and flowers,
reddish brown stems,
dark as the Japanese Maple
    in our garden.

Harilal, alert in his black *topi*,
about to return to work at the mill –
    a textile mill.

It is April or May 1941,
    in Ahmedabad, after lunch –
A day when Datta Khopker
    came by with his camera –

Here they are in the middle of life,
    their last child will be born this year –

Their eldest daughter watching from the doorway –

Who would have thought Harilal would die
    five years later –

The grandfather I never met.

Devibehn, I only knew as a widow,
                        forever in white –

If only Datta Khopker
        had taken more photographs –

of the garden, the street,
        of the house,
                of my mother –

If only Harilal had lived.

It's the same story:
        if only –

We pray to them now
        for our own lives –

I imagine they see me –
        Devibehn and Harilal
in Pennsylvania,
                surrounded by trees.

Green Acorns

Once again
I'm the seven-year-old girl
    who stood alone
  by the fence
in a school yard in New Orleans –
      beneath an oak tree –
Sun flickering shadows through leaves,
    sun twitching a lion's tail
      in the stillness –

My hands full of green acorns –
their smooth skins already scratched
and dug into by my nails –   Clear sap
sticky on my fingers –

The other girls ran away
as soon as they heard the music.
But I stayed and watched
and watched and didn't know
what it was I saw. My fists tightening
around those acorns, so the green
peeked out between my knuckles –
Did I understand anything?

For I know I gasped at the beautiful,
at the silky purple and black –
at the sun glinting on brass,
at the sparkling and shining everywhere
    on their old, creased faces –
I know I gasped at the slow,
  slow crooked dance –
a dance with earth itself, it seemed to me.

It was a small procession –
hadn't I just learnt to spell that word?
And the music: that sound
swept through me and around me
    and stayed.

Did I understand anything
          as I heard the beginning
of their song?   Their voices
so hoarse –   and I stood more
motionless than in 'freeze tag'
          and was numb
with looking at their tears
and their smiles full of grief –
numb with listening to a song
I wanted them to continue singing
and not stumble or hesitate –
as if my watching could help them
continue walking around the corner
          onto the next street.
And yet, I didn't want them to leave.

And still,
   I don't want them to go.

He Farms for Beauty

for Jane and Wolfgang Müller. Pennsylvania, 2003

He farms for beauty –
rents land from a doctor in town.

Land veined with darkness –
   white quartz rich soil.

Look at the short apple trees,
  deliberately stunted,
     all their strength diverted
into clusters of countless fruit.

Rows and rows of small branches
bent, almost distorted, with their burden of apples.

Today, the sunflowers stand like tomboys.
A tall, poised, cocksure stance –

  Here's a field
Persephone would have run into –

She would have worn a green dress
   or else a yellow one –

She would have hidden between such stalks and leaves.
She would have stayed between these sunflowers.

Dark heads camouflage bees –
bees burrowing down into spongy colours,
     soft browns and purples
streaked with ochre powder.

  And the broad leaves, rough
as a man's unshaven cheek –

Leaves on stems thrusting upwards,
upwards at each node

along the stalks.

Once cut,
these leaves wilt fast
        without water –
Look how even now the ones in your hands
    bow down with a dancer's gesture
                of limpness.

Each sunflower stands with so many
green arms hanging, elbows bent
        at sharp angles.

Tournesol,   girasol,

            surya-mukhi.

A thousand little suns
mirroring their Great Beloved
        in the sky –

Behind the sunflowers, another field –
behind that field, a wall of trees
rustling their early October colours –
Still so much green slowly giving way
to deep yellow and brown –
A rare flash of red lures birds –

And behind those woods,
blue, dark blue, azure mountains,
a haze of indigo, turquoise and lavender
against a watercolour, water-clean sky –

He farms for beauty –
This year the sunflowers are simply there
        for the sake of being there –

Next year, he says,
next year, I'll go for honey.

All afternoon
he works on a tombstone
for his dead neighbour –   the man wanted
his grave marked with a stone from his own yard.

Bees interrupt, making him look up
and turn towards the sunflowers –
His eyes unshielded, vulnerable
to the dust rising from the stone –
a huge slab, thick as a body.

The sunflowers wait –
Their petals, yellow blades that never fade –
One would think their round faces are prickly,
thorny with danger –   but no,
such softness cushions bees –

And the apples?
His wife picks them today
while Persephone watches
from the fields –

Phytoremediation

Do they gasp for air?
Pores choking on metallic dust
      for the lack of ozone –

Or do they choke on the idea
    of excessive ozone
 in mixed up atmospheres?

Bees crawl across their faces.

Do they gasp in pain?

Or is it joy? Are they drunk on sunlight,
      drunk on blue air?

Their greens and yellows reeling with the wind –

    These sunflowers, so tall, almost gawky,

        they are faster than Death.

    Undemanding queens –   What do they know?

Spartan beauties, I call them, sisters
of cacti, for they need so little, almost
    nothing from the soil.

Do they never tire of looking at the sun?

The sun over Chernobyl,
for example, where they live –
roots soaking up radioactive uranium –
      stems humming radioactive cesium,
   radioactive strontium – a chemical heat
buzzing with zeros –

What do they mean with their glances?
Their electric, burning glances –

           still beseeching bees,
   still daring birds to eat their seeds,
                     still glaring at the sky —
   Still egging on the sun —

Do Not Use the Word 'Erosion' Lightly

Rock-dust, sand, erosion –

Do not use the word 'erosion' lightly.

Remember the Gobi desert
    from school?

Flying over it, we see a train,
    and imagine such noise down there –

Noise buffered by sand, sand hushed by space –

Now it's endless sand.
        Seen from the skies
it's vaster than ever –

Do not call it 'golden',
    even if it is golden.

How many of us fly over it
    eating *kimchi* and rice?
How many of us
    will write about it?

Sand eats into Beijing,
and we think of bacteria, viruses –

Fever. Dried skin, dried fish –

Do not use these words lightly.

'We're all turning into deserts,'
says the girl next to me.

Must emptiness frighten?

This void is hypnotic.

Sand bruises and wounds
            your noble ideas –

What now?

Will you draw a circle
            around your soul?

Solo Piano: After Listening to Philip Glass

Death poems
are mere delusion –
Death is death.

Toko (1710–95)

You're so right, Toko,
death is death, and snow is snow –

Why write deluded poems?

Why ignore birth?

One year the winter solstice
revealed my daughter's
soon-to-be-born face to me.

But this year the darkness takes
the life of a man I should have met.

Basho's dream still wanders
over withered fields,

And I read Ryushi:

Man is Buddha –
the day and I
grow dark as one.

The piano is neutral:
a calm surgeon.

Snow falls and falls
and continues falling
for hours, seven hours, eight –

Snow falls as if some great goddess of the skies
were shaking feathers out of her hair –

Extravagant, her movements –
    as if driven by love and madness –

But are they feathers?
    Or flowers?

Large flakes –
    large as the largest roses, magnolias –

Wind blown –   these bright petals pile up fast,
    covering broken roots, bones –

Flowers that yearn to be birds –
the wind makes them swerve this way and that –

Feathers, flowers –
    now they fall like parachutes,
drift down the way some jellyfish sink,
    drawn into the current –

And how well the piano knows this:
    falling snow, solstice darkness,
texture of a skull's forehead –

Snow falls and falls
filling up the open mouth
    of a dead man.

Thickness and wetness in the air,
    and yet, lightness,
as the wind cuts through –

While elsewhere
    women watch their children
    from kitchen windows.

Whose turn is it now
    to tell a story?

Secluded but happy in its being,
    the piano brings back
memories of a girl in a long black coat,
    a red scarf around her neck and throat,
leading a black Labrador through the snow.

Notes

1 '*And look: the olives ripen, the lizards stretch.*' This title is the last line from Eleanor Wilner's poem, 'Αυτίο, Cassandra', from her book, *The Girl with Bees in Her Hair*, (Copper Canyon Press, 2004). Αυτίο is demotic Greek for 'goodbye'.

2 'The Smell of Lilacs'. I am indebted to Dieter Kühn for his excellent study, *Schillers Schreibtisch in Buchenwald* (S. Fischer Verlag, 2005), which provided much of the information and inspiration for this poem. Charlotte's letter, quoted in this poem, is my translation from the original.

3 Thanks also to Michael Augustin and Walter Weber for their three-hour radio documentary, *Ein Abend für Friedrich Schiller*, broadcast by Radio Bremen.